About the Author

Norman Kowalskie was raised like a postcard, growing up in America, living in Europe and being born in the Middle East, his life has been rooted in the wind. Never having a sense of home or identity, his life as an immigrant on whichever continent he was living in at the time had a reality of racism and prejudice! Yet, in his heart, he is an American. Impregnated with Hollywood and pop music in his youth, he spent his teenage years living with a love for the American dream only to be struck down by life, fate and addiction!

Confessions of a Unicorn

Norman Kowalskie

Confessions of a Unicorn

Olympia Publishers
London

www.olympiapublishers.com
OLYMPIA PAPERBACK EDITION

Copyright © Norman Kowalskie 2024

The right of Norman Kowalskie to be identified as author of this work has been asserted in accordance with sections 77 and 78 of the Copyright, Designs and Patents Act 1988.

All Rights Reserved

No reproduction, copy or transmission of this publication may be made without written permission.
No paragraph of this publication may be reproduced, copied or transmitted save with the written permission of the publisher, or in accordance with the provisions of the Copyright Act 1956 (as amended).

Any person who commits any unauthorised act in relation to this publication may be liable to criminal prosecution and civil claims for damage.

A CIP catalogue record for this title is available from the British Library.

ISBN: 978-1-80074-370-0

This is a work of fiction.
Names, characters, places and incidents originate from the writer's imagination. Any resemblance to actual persons, living or dead, is purely coincidental.

First Published in 2024

Olympia Publishers
Tallis House
2 Tallis Street
London
EC4Y 0AB

Printed in Great Britain

Dedication

I dedicate this book to my dear mother, the most supreme and sublime energy this world has ever seen. Thank you, mother!

Acknowledgements

Thanks to my dear family who have supported me through my life. Thanks to my dear sister for always picking up the pieces. Thanks to my dear brothers for being a part of my life. Thanks to all my friends, especially my one and only lawyer, for always working for free and for your company throughout this life. Thanks to blabaratzu for all the confusion! And last but not least, thank you, my dear unicorn friend, for showing me how to dream!

For Soraya

Chapter 1

Sparkle's Stars and Rainbows

The night is young dear friend one pirate said to the other, our gold is sunk but our barrels are still full of rum and drink. They grin at each other, then one pulls out a dagger and stabs the other one in the neck. With blood gushing out of his eyes, mouth and ears, he falls to the ground. Crawling and reaching for his mother on the deck of the ship, he somehow manages to grab a bucket and throw it at his opponent, which does not really harm him but does very much piss him off. Being the nasty pirate he is, he throws his dagger to the floor and goes on to choke the other pirate on the deck. Little to his attention behind him is a rat who now has a dagger sticking in the middle of its body as he dies slowly. That was in the year 1739, and I am the reincarnation of that rat! A good two hundred and eighty years have passed, and I find myself in the middle of a European city screaming and mostly being screamed at by the ducking love of my life. She is sitting on a curb and it is cold, fucking cold it is. We both want nothing more yet dread the moment where we burn money through a pipe. At the moment we smoke coke all day every day and this is what we are waiting for!

The man bringing it to us is…well, let's just call him King Kong because he is big, black and has all our… well actually her money.

"I never needed this, I never wanted this, you know that I am a self-destructing queen and an animal of addiction," she screams while she cries her tears out on the cold and dark sidewalk.

The sobbing continues. I myself have always been a monster of addiction, never knew anything else. The beginning of my time was a drug-infested den, and the bear living in it amongst us, ruling it with an iron fist, was my father, but we will get to that later. Have you ever seen a black leaf hanging on a tree in autumn that's about to die? Or smoke curling away from one's cigarette as the proprietor is falling asleep! Well, that, in theory, was the fading yet never-ending cycle/bond this woman and I have, as I always called it, an agreement of freedom. I cannot emphasise how strong this is or was back then, for all I do is tell the story of how two Unicorns met each other!

Down the path behind her on the sidewalk, like the few dozen times it had happened in the past weeks, you can see a dark figure… getting closer and closer; this man is our King Kong. Every time this happens something dies inside me. It's not the melancholic drug addict prick in me. For a drug addiction comes at one's own hand and reasoning. No, in fact on the one hand I thrive on the fact that we will smoke cocaine through a pipe soon. On the other hand, one must understand the pure madness, filth, misery and sorrow this woman goes through just by putting up with me. It takes two to tango, they say, but if you pull a person out of the jungle and put them into a disco, then it truly is unfair to expect them to keep up, especially if they are willing to pay for all the fun.

"There is no victim in this crime, you melodramatic cunt!" she looks at me and screams! "Get your head out of your ass and stop crying about what we are. It's time to get this behind us."

She is not a mean woman or one to be unkind, but when she starts something, she tends to go the whole nine yards; that is why

I ducking love her. The darkness behind King Kong fades as he gets closer. Although drug dealers are mostly rotten cunts, this one had a heart somewhere between his head and his wallet. As he sees me, standing a little paralyzed and full of self-loathing, with her on the footpath crying, he starts to walk faster!

"What is, what is problem, up, up, why you do this? This no okay!" he said.

His English was never really good. We quickly wipe our faces free and start walking alongside him. No drug dealer is free of paranoia, especially a black one.

"Why make problem? Why cry? People watch this!" he said.

At this point, he was seriously concerned! They start walking in front of me as I follow behind them up the street. Try explaining to this African man that your self-indulging drug addiction has locked you in a masochistic cage and you are trying to get out of it. However, my Unicorn friend was always better at explaining something my big mouth could not explain, even with a thousand words. And so she did in a manner that was quiet and took about four to five street blocks.

King Kong was, in reality, a businessman, and his answer was: "Why you come, one time, or two, three, four time sometime in one night? Buy big and this not happen again! Then you no come and come, again and again, understand?"

I was walking behind them but I could hear them clearly and thought to myself of course 'buy big'. Why didn't I think of that myself! A normal buy in bulk so I can make more money and don't have to spend the whole winter on the streets freezing my ass off philosophy. I could have said this to him. Unfortunately, a businessman does not understand the various dynamics that make a Unicorn a Unicorn! The tendency of a monster is to keep coming back to bug, scare and irritate his prey! Besides the fact that it does not fucking matter if you have one gram or ten. You smoke it all until there is nothing left. The deal is done, I'm sitting in a taxi which King Kong has winked from around the corner, as he puts her into the taxi, we both look at him, he can see it in our eyes, we don't have a cent left to our name. At this moment he pulls out ten euros and gives it to the driver, with confusion the driver looks at us and asks us where we are going. Shortly after typing it into his navigation, he starts driving. I sometimes recall what that cab looked like from behind as King Kong watched it drive off. Was it his way of ensuring that his costumers don't get caught on the way home? Was it his heart that put us in the taxi and paid it? A mix of both, maybe? Probably a mix, with a fucked up sense of premonition for what we are to him.

Silence hits us like an explosion from the sky. Calmness was never something that lasted long in my life. 'Tis, in fact, one of the things me and my unicorn friend had in common; she was more quiet than me, used words with sublime precision and accuracy. Almost like there was a forest inside her breaking apart tree after tree, with rampaging animals, burning leaves and screaming insects, a natural mess exploding and spitting out a tiny little leaf at the end of the valley at the foot of the forest. She had a lot going on inside! The few words that would come out every now and then were liquid gold. Me and her had that in common, a war, a civil war going on inside of us, one our forefathers had started long before us just to be passed unto the next generation.

European cities are very deserted and peaceful at night. People don't live at night here; if they do, they hide indoors. Not much was said in the taxi. We both knew what was going to happen soon, so that brought a tiny moment of silence into us. It is a drug addict's job to mourn the minutes passing, to count them going by, to await the next fix, hit, kick or bellyache until he or she goes looking for the next one. And so it was for the rest of the taxi ride until we pulled up to the street where we both lived at the moment. Paying a taxi cab and getting out of one was always a very hasty and fast act for me, as was running up the stairs so you could get to your compadre the 'pipe'. However, my dear Unicorn friend was much calmer at such ethics than I was. She had that in her, do not ask me why. Inside, she was torn up like a tornado, outside in such harmony; it was for someone like me, very soothing to see. Yet the junkie in us never stood still! Especially when we had coke in our pockets.

I ran up the stairs, she walked. The door to our apartment was very old and could be knocked open by a strong wind, although both of us at times were very paranoid, we never much cared for what happened to our safety or bodies. Being raised without a geographic or personal identity does something to your standard of safety. I wait for her to open the door, and as we step into the flat, even I get calmer! Getting closer to your utensils does something to a Fein, it calms you somehow. Just the sheer fact that you will get high soon, be it for just a worn-down version of a minute, makes you nonetheless slow down. If you rush through the few minutes it takes to get high, then all you've got left are the empty and full of spasm-filled tense hour or so it takes you to score again, and that is, even for a 'rush through junkie' like myself, unbearable.

The first thing that greets us is our roommate Hiroshima, a Brokeback Japanese diva, in other words, a cat I had acquired from the southern parts of Europe. She always showed up when there was something to consume, mostly because the attention was absorbed away from her. She quickly disappears into a corner and continues to clean herself, not that we start to think that she liked hanging out with us! My dear Unicorn friend throws her rucksack onto a small green kitchen table and goes into the bathroom. The silence in the room or any part of our path together was always nice. In a way, I think she knew that I badly needed any kind of calmness or peace. Silence is a rare thing for me, just doesn't happen much, but in her presence, a supreme energy ruled over me! Even if it pained me sometimes, it was in retrospect the nicest pain I ever had. After she got out of the bathroom, we started right away. Sometimes I would cook the coke and sometimes she would cook it. It did not matter if we needed it or wanted it every day. The fact was we did it every day. Neither of us were people that did not share, and so it was with the destructive monsters we had inside ourselves; we wanted to share them with each other.

The first hit of the session is always the best, everything after that is like running after a freight train with a bicycle... useless! If it had been up to her, we would have waited longer to take the second or third hit, but I wanted to dance, I wanted to see the devil laugh in our faces, spit in his hand and smear it on my face. I was a junkie long before her. Don't get me wrong, she loved it, as nature has it though women are in a lot of things, smarter than men are. And before you dance with the devil, it is smarter to prep yourself, or at least dress up a little bit. Not let him stick it right in you without warning or lubricant of any kind. That was how I did it. However, smoking with her was like drinking wine with a Frenchman right in the middle of some divine vineyard. If there was a chance in hell to smoke coke like that, then it was only with her, next to her. During the session we would laugh, talk or cry a little bit depending on what we were talking about. Sometimes we would smoke it in bed, but most of the time, it was done in the kitchen. Looking back on it now, she was, without doubt, the best company to smoke with; this I know for sure.

A crack high drops like the whiskey glass of an old man who has just had a stroke, breaking into a thousand pieces without warning. Afterwards, we usually went out and got more, and there were some nights where we would compensate it with alcohol, pills or something else to help us calm down. However, this night was different. I thought that after the scene on the street earlier that night, she would be pissed off or angry after the coke was gone, but she wasn't. She knew how much of this endeavour was mine or hers to burden, she knew a Unicorn had nothing and no one to blame but itself. We went up to a loft bed we had in a small yet 'filled up to the brim with stuff' room. It was our den, the place we would always shake of stuff together. After rolling a cigarette full of weed, I put on a record and crawled up to the bed, and we lay next to each other.

She was kind in times of sorrow. I do not know if it were the fact that she knew I would bleed with self-disgust for never being able to stop myself or her from going back time after time, for not being strong enough to stop any bad habit I had or for being a little tiny withering Unicorn lying in his own piss. I think she was just kind because she liked being next to me in such a rotten state. She understood that for me in those moments, I was torn in between reality, not because of myself, I never gave a fuck about myself. It was her I cared for and her who gave me hope that there was something left inside of me to save. In truth, I feared for her wellbeing a number of times, but that would dissipate fast. She went through more difficult problems in her life than having some melodramatic Unicorn friend show her a way of burning money through a pipe. Next to her, in those moments while Tom Waits or some other record would play in the background, as we very slowly started touching each other. There in between us, under our blankets, a sun would slowly rise. In a dark place far and beyond where there is no spark in all sight to be seen, only feral creatures play. A brightness would appear. Sparks would fly with every touch we laid upon each other, even a drug addict needs to see a light at the end of the tunnel, and that was ours. The record stopped playing, and there was that sound of a needle retracting from the vinyl and sitting back down at the start position. I leaned up, rubbed my face with my hands and looked around for my tobacco.

I was rolling a cigarette as I felt her place her fingers on the lower back part of my arm. Not all her fingers, just three, the fourth one along with her thumb would barely touch my body. If I could explain to you how a second turns into a moment which is then stretched into eternity where you forget who and why you are, I would, but it would be a futile attempt. There is no explaining what it feels like when a Unicorn touches you!

"Will you flip the record, or should I climb down?" she asked.

"I will," I said.

"And my tobacco, can you give it to me?" she asked.

"Yes," I said.

She never asked if there were something wrong, she would feel it and then ask me with a look!

"I am sorry," I said.

"For what?" she asked.

"For being this fucked up shadow of myself, for being a goddamn train wreck, for bringing all this into your life, into your home," I said.

"Turn the record over, please," she said.

And so I did. I came back up, and she had already fallen

asleep. She never slept with a cigarette in her fingers, it would always be in the ashtray half-smoked with the smoke curling away. I never would fall asleep fast, not ever before she would fall asleep. Since I was a child, I had never needed more than three to four hours sleep, sometimes even less. In the past years, my sleeping problems had gotten much worse. Due to all the serious drug abuse and party binging, sleep was something I had to pay an expensive price for.

But I am not completely sure that this was the reason I would not fall asleep before her. I think I just liked to fall asleep long after her so I could watch and listen to her sleep. There is nothing more beautiful than watching a Unicorn sleep. We never said stuff like 'you have a pretty rainbow coming out behind you while you fly around'. Or that, 'the stars shine bright while you gallop in the mist'. It was too tacky! We weren't those kind of Unicorns. Our feelings for each other were always very vivid. We just knew. Besides the fact that a Unicorn knows that there are not many creatures who can put up or, better yet, bear its rare yet arrogant presence. So a Unicorn can't be picky. However, they are still creatures who like to be smothered with compliments or praised by anyone not, while they are awake or can hear you. For the love of Mingus that will make a Unicorn run in the other direction. It wants to hear sweet nothings whispered in its ear, smothered by beauty from a distance!

And so I waited until she was sound asleep so I could fill her ears with nothings and somethings, so I could whisper my compulsive confessions repeatedly in her ear until I was so tired that I would attempt to sleep. But it never worked; I could never sleep with my head resting on the back of a Unicorn! She makes sounds when she sleeps, tiny little ones, little breaths. I don't know why, I don't know what they mean, I just know I understand them all. For some reason only Mingus knows, I would wait until she made some sounds or fall asleep waiting on them... I rolled another cigarette.

Does she need you? Does a monster need the dark? Does a Unicorn need a rainbow?

I can never say that I made it to anything. There are many people that kick their habits, I was not one of them. Not everyone wallows in their own filth like a pig, and if they do they tend to learn from it. Not me; I am just another junkie, just another waste of time and space, never listened to anyone, never listened to myself. Just could not bear the pain I had on my shoulders, one I had made completely on my own, so I decided to throw it on my loved ones. Like a china man overworked and under lived going out to take the trash out to the alley, he decides to throw it into a dumpster already full of shit from the past weeks. I, too, decided to pile my shit over more shit, just to lay myself between it all and watch my life further grow on the garbage. All that was ever good in my life was brought out by her, who decided to dig through it, find me and rejuvenate what was left of me. I who decided to finally rid this world of my pathetic existence and submerge myself with the filth I had made in my life. For Mingus's sake, it was she who saw the Unicorn in me; it was she who showed me my first rainbow! Not the other way around!

Something is wrong here, my cigarette is done, something is wrong, something grows, I've seen it before, I've felt it before, something goes, something is here, I know this gold I have seen it before, I have felt it before!

I know this can grow, but something is wrong! All my life there was always something wrong. Never full, never asleep, never alone. Never at the end, get wrong, get right, get it seventy-eight thousand miles away from Meeeeeeee!

But then something good tonight, something good you turned away from. Something good you touched, afterward, after all that we sleep upon, we lie upon, she makes the moves, the moves to send me there into something not wrong. She makes the moves that lay stars over rainbows... I am tired now!

Chapter 2

The Grinding Mill

I scream in my sleep, always have. Long before my drug abuse years this started. I never understood why but yet again, who understands anything that happens in sleep time. Maybe it was just my way of fighting against everything!

"My heart sinks when you scream," she said, we were still in bed.

"Did I scream again?" I asked.

"Yes," she said.

"How bad?" I asked.

"Bad, really bad," she said.

I rolled her a cigarette. She was the kindest person to sleep next to. All she needed was a cigarette to wake with. It was ten in the morning, and my mind started counting hours. Living in a desert of substance abuse was not easy. I knew that soon I had to leave my sanctuary to find another oasis for the day, for I had a problem she did not have, Heroin! Sleep a few hours and then get up and run around trying to borrow some money. Hmmm, I was thinking. It's not difficult to read a smackhead's mind; there is only one thing going on up there…

"What is it?" she asked.

"Nothing," I said.

She did not even bother to ask further; she always knew, I knew she knew! Shame is the trap a heroin addict sets for himself.

I laid back down and tried to get some more sleep. When you're a little sick and you know that you might find something later, your mind kind of shuts the fuck up; it's like feeding a ten-year-old French fries in a pool of ketchup. I woke up periodically until it was three in the afternoon. She stayed asleep. I put on my clothes and left my swamp paradise. Hiroshi was the only one to see me leave. I closed the door behind me and remembered what a good friend once said to me; it's never too late to start again, so don't dwell on what is yet to be. I walked down the steps, and the first step I took outside reminded me of the dream I had last night.

I was lying in a dark room, just married, the birth of my firstborn just washed in the next room. As I entered the room, I saw doctors surrounding my child; it was a mess of blood and puss. From every corner I could see nurses running around with equipment and sharp tools. I pushed the doctors aside and saw a Unicorn kneeling on the floor, and it was dying. I overheard the doctors saying that this was not right, it's been thirteen hours and we still can't save him.

The Unicorn looked at me and said,

"Am I a good offering? Will you ever get clean?"

All of a sudden the doctors disappeared and ran in every direction; the nurses were long gone, a clown pushed his way through all the doctors and started devouring the beast while blood ran and slopped around his mouth. He screamed, "My lover, my killer."

I didn't know what to make of it, but I have weird dreams all the time, so it didn't really bother me. I had more important things to do. No one trusted me anymore, I had barely any connections left, King Kong didn't fuck around with smack, so I had to improvise. I could not beg anyone for money anymore, so I decided to hit the street and ask someone if I could run along with him and buy off his dealer, which meant I would probably need to pay a little more!

I needed some cash. At the moment, it was winter and people here barely use their bikes! The plan was to let my way into some building corridor and see if I could get lucky and find a bike or two to take to some pawnshop. My appearance from the outside still looked kind of okay, so I decided to go to a big office building and see if any of those middle-class fuckers left their bikes lying around somewhere.

All of a sudden, I got a call. I looked at my phone and saw that it was my older brother; he probably needed me to drive somewhere, pick something up and drop it off again! It was a good gig a year or two ago, but I hadn't gotten asked for a long while now, not only due to the fact that I was just never reachable nowadays but also because I nodded off one too many times behind the steering wheel, it got expensive to fix the car every other time I half crashed it into something.

Besides, I needed to get high. My nose was running, and I had maybe two hours until I was in full withdrawal. I wasn't about to let that happen. I was about to get into the tram when I saw a building door open and some housekeeper outside cleaning, brushing leaves from the steps. I decided to make my move. I walked fast and went right past her. She gave me a stare and a long frown. I didn't have time to sweet-talk her, I am sure she will come looking soon. I ran down into the basement and saw that even the door to the bike cellar was opened, she must have just finished cleaning it. This is my lucky fucking day! Now I just have to get past that housekeeper with preferably two bikes; the more the fucking better! I grabbed the easiest two to carry and ran up the stairs again; she was waiting for me the minute I got up there. She was a thick-headed, probably Serbian woman by the look of her. She immediately grabs one of the bikes, yanks around on it and screams at the top of her lungs. I wasn't in the mood, I shoved the bike down the stairs, and the housekeeper flew down with it. I have no idea if she made it or not. I jumped on the bike and rode it to the pawnshop!

If there was a prize for the biggest scumbag award, I am sure I could compete with the best of them, that back there was only the tip of the iceberg. There were four people waiting in line at the pawnshop. The minute I was up, I could see the dude's face, he knew me, and all he was thinking of was no, no fucking way am I going to put up with this guy again. It must have been my tenth bike in the past week!

I already bent my head with a, "come on man, please, just one more time," look on my face.

"Another bike!" is his first comment.

"It's the last one I have, please help me out." I said.

"Look I… I can't," he said.

I don't know what it was. I can't tell you if he looked at me and could see that I was about to start crying, I had lost everything, my dignity was leaking out of my ass, all my self-esteem was long gone, and not one sparkle in my eye.

He just looked at the floor and said, "How much are you looking to sell it for?"

I said "Dude, forty bucks, and it's yours."

I will give you thirty for it," he said.

Normally I would have been pissed off, but I was an inch away from shitting my pants and vomiting on the floor. I took the thirty euros and ran towards a friend's place. I knew I could score there. I knew he had something. He had told me not to come over any more because last time he let me in, I was sick and begged him for some. I don't give a fuck; I need to score. His place was not far from the pawnshop. I jumped into the next bus and got out at the third stop, and there were two Christians, young ones standing next to the bus stop handing tickets out for god. They reached out to give me one of the pamphlets, and I just walked right past them.

Please be home, please, for Mingus's sake, be the fuck home. I didn't have his number anymore, so I couldn't call him if I wanted to. He made me erase it from my phone in front of him with that last escapade we went through. I had to knock on his door and get lucky. I had to stand outside of his door for a few minutes, thinking about how I should announce myself to him. It could be that he tells me to get lost right away. But standing there and being minutes away from serious withdrawal did something to me; it was not the fact that I was about to beg him again to let me in, but just the fact that I had let everything spiral so far down to this bottomless pit I call a person, myself! I used to have a young man's body. I used to be free. How did it get this far again and again? Why have I turned my life into a prison, with the key to freedom in my own hands? Where did it go wrong? My life has turned into a cotton candy nightmare of Freudian invention, just recalling the last two hours of it shakes me to my very core. Enough! Ring this fucking bell and get things over with.

I ring the bell, and he just buzzes me in. I was very surprised… I walk up to the fourth floor of the building and stand in front of the door, and he opens it with a very weird look on his face. He must have thought I was someone else.

"Were you expecting someone else?" I said.

"Yes, I just ordered some food. I thought you were the delivery guy!" he replied.

"Can I come in?" I asked.

He shrugs his shoulders and I pass swiftly through the door. He closes it right behind me.

"Do you have money?" he asked.

"Yes!" I replied.

"Okay," he said.

As I sit down I can see that he either had a cleaning lady clean his apartment or that he had maybe paid someone in smack to do it! There were enough people who would take on the job of cleaning a heroin dealer's apartment for money!

"Did you clean the place?" I asked.

"No, I had a girl do it… what do you need?" he said.

"Just one gram, please!" I said.

I was surprised he didn't ask, didn't even really care that I had rung his bell. Maybe it was my face, it takes a junkie to know a junkie, but I didn't care much for the answer. All I could see was the sparkles about to go inside of me. The deal is done. He let me get high in his apartment, and I was gone as fast as I had arrived. The smile you have on your face is not visible to the world while you walk around right after you have gotten high. It's not a physical one, it's hidden under your lips, kind of just on the corner of your lips somewhere. Nonetheless, I was satisfied, and the fact was my head was going to be calm until I had to shake it off again. I have enough things to do in life. I could be somewhere enjoying the sights, or just cleaning up my room from forgotten memories that hang down my walls at night, maybe looking for a job, but none of that is ever a priority. I shall always kill the hours to come in a corner somewhere dripping and nodding off, like drops of a milky hinge long rusted to the bones. It's not the divine obstacle of death I am afraid of; it's life that scares me!

Chapter 3

History

I was born far from the place I was living in at the moment. There was a war while I was in my mother's belly, a bad one, not that there are any good wars, but this one took its toll on the people and land. It had started a good seven years before I was born. I don't remember any of the screams, tears or bombs, but I feel their echo to this day! It was at the climax of the war and in another city far away from where the war was, lived an uncle of mine who, a week before I was due to come out of my mother, had burned in a fire. The war was only in a city much further south of where we lived at that time. In desperate times people do desperate things, and at that time the price of fuel was fluctuating rapidly. So one would buy it and store it when it was cheap, and so did my uncle. My father got the news on the telephone that his brother had an accident and had died! No one can really explain what he did to have the fuel in his house explode, but it wasn't important. Once my mother got the news, she went into shock and out came me a week early.

    A few days after that, my father announced the fact that he was planning to travel and see to his brother's remains, and my mother decided it would be best if we all went. The train we took was the last train to ever leave that station. The hospital, along with most of the city and the train station, was crushed into dust by all the destruction the war brought! I was told that we could feel the tremors in the train. Maybe some people wonder why their parents left the place they were raised in. I am sure that some people even blame their parents for leaving. If only crumbs are left of the place you were born and raised, then I understand if one chooses to leave! All these occasions happened swiftly and promptly. The hand of destiny does not work in slow motion; when she hits, she usually tends to come down like dominos. And so it was.

We were smitten by all these overwhelming and devastating events. No one really wanted to talk. There was so much to be said, but first, we needed to let all these pictures and scenes, yet to be frozen as memories, settle in and digest into what will later become history! Due to a political coup and severe change in religious belief, my parents could no longer tolerate the situation that was slowly but surely taking over their beloved country. It took them a good year and some liquidating to be able to even think about going in a direction. We left in a crazy haste; it's not easy leaving a country with a one-year-old and three other kids. It took us a while to work out the details, but we left as quickly as we could. The country we lived in was not an easy country to leave; you had to flee from it. There was not really time to plan but my mother was the smarter one of the two. So she chose which direction to head, and that was as far north in Europe as we could get, preferably Sweden or England, she knew that there was no way of ever making a solid plan when you are fleeing a country in that state. But if you aim for Germany, you would probably end up in Greece or some other Balkan country, and that was not going to happen to us.

I was barely a year old and I cannot, for the life of me, remember any part of that journey. I just know these crumby details and these sprinkles of information. Yet all these events still ring their bell over my present-day memories. They say those first years are the most important ones, if that is true, then they were stolen from me and replaced by someone's idea of a sovereign state, for my present-day person has a black corner down in the bowels of my memory where all this is stored.

After settling into Europe and just taking a few years to let everything sink in, we slowly started to get the feeling that both our feet were maybe starting to touch the ground. It takes time for everything to fall into place. Even when they do, they kind of scatter and kind of fall into any place that fits. We lived in a small apartment, all the children in one room, and my parents slept next to the living room. I spent most of my time outside, you see, inside, was a very steady and chaotic downfall of my father's mood, which he was in, any particular day. One day was not the same as the next, and the only steady thing was my father's daily heroin abuse. Once he started selling from the apartment, the place turned into a fucking coffee shop. Don't get me wrong, he was in a great mood in the morning right after his first hit, but that would decline in a matter of minutes. So outside was kind of the best-case scenario for me.

My memory starts with my father's drug abuse and business; after all, he would take me with him so it would be safer in the car on the way to his connection. I was a young boy with very big brown eyes, and anytime someone looked into the car, they were immediately distracted by me. I don't know how much of that sunk into my father's memory or even how sorry he felt for me or any of us. I always got the impression that to him, it sufficed just to be the donator of sperm. He didn't care that one day I would grow into an adult and remember all these things. That I would one day piece together the puzzle. As a matter of fact, play with spoons and lighters myself. This is of no interest to someone who is looking out for their own addiction. And so it was for the rest of the time we spent there with him. The violence got worse, and the drug abuse grew and grew. Today I am a full-grown Unicorn, and I understand what it means to have a never-ending story tattooed in your brain called 'addiction'. However, if you have a problem with this world, you tend to want to solve it, and the more I look back, the more I find out that this problem began long before I did.

As soon as we could, by 'we', I mean my mother and siblings, we packed our bags and fled, yet again. This time it wasn't from a country or a regime but from our own home, a kind of 'poetic injustice' if you will, lies not in your heart, but the lion's den, so-called home. My father tried to stop us, but after being horribly abused by years of his smoke, needles and just plain misery, my mother had grown a very sincere and thick outer shell. She didn't pack when he was asleep, and she didn't sneak around. She waited until he was wide awake and full of sparkles, all happy and shining from his morning fix. Just so he could watch us leave. No screaming, yelling or breaking of things could derail my mother from her goal of leaving that old rotten junkie! And so it was that we left for America.

Chapter 4

The Essence of It All

Nirvana must be a lonely place, I've never been there, but it seems to me no one ever stays there long. If one reaches this state of enlightenment, said to be the epiphany of all those weird places. Then what? Do you go running for the next level of sublime whatever the fuck! That would be my first guess. You can't blame a Buddhist monk for chasing the next fix, as a fiend has the freedom to play a never-ending game. So does anyone else, no matter what the medium is, that helps him or her cross over to the other side. Bringing me to my point, which is scoring something! My Unicorn friend and I had just met a dark figure we called King Kong, but he either didn't have time or just didn't trust us enough to pick up the phone every time I called him. I was alone, and I had this... well, you can't really call them a connection! They were just two smackheads living in an apartment you didn't even want to look at, let alone spend time in.

I called them itchy and scratchy because one itched while the other would always scratch.

Achhhh! I couldn't look at myself anymore and everything was just pissing me off. There must be wheels churning somewhere to this machine we call life. Because sometimes something is just stuck in between the gears. It's always a surprise when I go and visit itchy and scratchy; their apartment was on the top floor of some run-down building. I knocked on the door and at first I heard nothing… then some scrambling of sorts. After that, a very squeaky voice asked who it was!

"It's me, open up," I said!

He opens the door, and the first thing I notice is that he is holding smoke in his lungs! After he closes the door behind me, I go in only to see a pipe in the middle of the floor, I turn around and he blows out a bunch of smoke. They always did everything on the floor. They had furniture, but no one in their right mind would ever sit on it! Everything they had fit into that tiny little space between all the rotten furniture, and apparently they had just figured out how to smoke coke!

He sits down and grabs out from next to the pipe an extension lead with several sockets in it. He then scrambles around looking for something, eventually he finds an old Nokia cell phone and starts tearing it apart. Meanwhile, I hear someone flush the toilet behind me. Out comes the other part of this legendary duo, a girl. She had flushed the toilet, but on her face, arms and eyes, you could see that she had just shot up. At that point I had to interrupt this endeavour of his. Her face made me jealous!

"Do you have anything on you," I asked?

"Wait, wait!" he said.

"Come on, man, I don't got much time. What the fuck are you doing anyway?" I said.

At this moment, the girl behind me, who was obviously not as paranoid as he was, answered:

"He is trying to rig the microphone out of the cell phone into the socket, so he can spy on our neighbours!" she said in a very slow and doped-up voice.

"They are fucking spying on us, not the other way around!

And I am going to catch them in the act. They think they can fuck with us? I will show them. Where the fuck is the flat head screwdriver?" he said.

"Dude, can you please let me score? I got money," I said.

"Just a second," he said.

"Besides, man, how the fuck are you going to ever get that inside of your neighbour's place? Did you ever think of that? Hugh!" I said.

"Let me fucking work! I'll get it in there somehow. I'll break down their door, IF I FUCKING HAVE TO!" he said.

He made himself another hit and got out his scale; she was nodding off in the corner. I wanted to leave as fast as I could, not to mention the fact that the place was just a scum's paradise! I was slowly but surely starting to get paranoid myself.

I came to myself on a bench, somewhere around the corner from itchy and scratchies place. I don't remember where I got high! Suddenly my phone rang, but it took me a while to find it; I was still out of it and at the same time I was trying to lite a cigarette. By the time I had it in my mouth and found the phone, it had already stopped ringing. I nodded off again and had a daydream about Joseph Stalin pouring cement on a car I was about to get into! He was standing on top of it with a grin on his face. I get closer, and he looks at me with the cement all hard around the car and says, "now you can go slower!" I was woken up again by my phone ringing, this time I got to it before it stopped!

It was my Unicorn friend, she said I needed to come home and that another friend was waiting on me there because he needed a driver! I knew right away who it was, Monkey! A big German fellow, the type of person with a liver of steel. Germans can drink in general, but this guy tends to push every limit to its crude maximum. I gathered myself and headed home as fast as I could.

Once I got home, I saw that Monkey was sitting at the kitchen table. My Unicorn friend had a pipe in front of her, and Monkey was vigilantly waiting for her to finish cooking so they could smoke. I got jealous, very jealous not only of the fact that she was cooking without me but also because the man we had just met, King Kong, obviously picked up her call and not mine earlier!

"Where did you get that from?" I asked.

"Take one guess." She replied.

Of course he picks up her phone call. I thought to myself. I was a rotten snake in his eyes; he knew that most of the money came from her. I always begged and pleaded with him for a better price or just to front it to me.

"Monkey, let's talk!" I said.

He was irritated but still came into my room with me.

"What's up?" I asked.

"We need to drive to Spain!" he said.

My brother had just bought a farm down there, the Spaniards called it a finka!

"How much time do I have?" I asked.

"The sooner, the better." He replied.

I was the only one with a driver's license, therefore always the driver for every important event. However, nothing else was going through my mind than the fact I needed a bunch of smack to get me through this twenty-hour drive.

"What are we taking down there?" I asked.

"A car full of stuff!" he said.

Monkey knew what was going through my head. He gave me one look and said:

"How much money do you need?"

"150, no wait, 200 euros!" I said.

He gave me the money and I left the apartment. The

spontaneous planning of all this and the running around didn't bother me. I never planned further than the next sparkle or rainbow. As a matter of fact, permanent anything made me nervous concerning life, that is. A job or plan of any kind was never my strength. On the contrary, if I think of the next years of my life or can see them planned out, I get nervous, very nervous! All I see at that point is me flying over all of it with an army of horses underneath me, trampling over it, leaving nothing but ruins in the dust. Oh no, sir, not me, I must disagree. Goodbye horses!

I had everything I needed. It didn't take me long; I just had to call the right people. With money, the right people are the ones you want to call! I took a cab to the outskirts of town where the car was waiting for me, with Monkey inside it. When I got to the car, I could see that it was packed full to the brim with luggage and equipment. Monkey was digging around on the floor next to the driver's seat. I got in, and I could see that he was trying to scratch some lines together out of a bag.

Make me one too, I said and started the car. Monkey was not a smackhead like I was, he didn't say no to the occasional line, but in the car, it was just coke he was sniffing! I wanted to say goodbye to my dear Unicorn companion, so I drove home with the excuse that I needed to get my lucky charm, a fat rubber duck! I wasn't a superstitious man, but the rubber duck was! And he would not have forgiven me if I drove to Spain without him. The minute I got home, I went into her room and saw that she was sleeping. Hiroshima, my cat, was the only one half-awake. I loved to watch her when she was asleep; nothing is more beautiful than a resting Unicorn. I gave her a long stare and whispered into the air, "I miss you when you're not around," then I left quietly.

Chapter 5

Mingus is God

I will never be able to explain to anyone what it is that makes a normal person turn into a drug fiend. All the theories can get fucked when you are in a downward spiral you slowly and steadily built with your own hands! A great empire of filth, which you watched grow into a very bad habit. All I know is, if a man can become a monster, then a monster can become a man! We had been on the road for about twelve hours. I had to stop here and there to make sure I could get high in the different service stations we would pass. For the moment, it was fine. My nerves were calm as long as I could soothe my cravings. I knew that this wave of content would collapse at one point, I had not slept for days, and we still had about eight hours to drive.

Monkey was asleep in the back seat. I started throwing empty cans at his face, so I would have someone to talk to. The Spanish landscape escaping time after time in the rearview mirror was so beautiful that it was pissing me off!

"Wake the fuck up, you cunt. This is no way to treat your driver."

I was at the climax of my sleep deprivation. He woke up with an unbelievably confused and troubled face. "Where are we?" he asked.

"I am the driver, not the navigator. I've just been heading south; if I had to guess, I would say somewhere in the northern part of Spain."

He digs around for a beer, cracks it open and drinks it down as if it was an elixir to heal him from all the painful sleep he had just gone through!

"What are we listening to? Is that Spanish radio?"

"That's Mingus!"

"Oh Jesus, not Mingus again."

"Not Jesus, God, Mingus is god, Monkey!"

He crawled into the front seat and settled in as if he was about to get lectured.

"I never asked why, why Mingus, why is Mingus god?"

"Well, Monkey, I am glad you asked. Get out your bag, scratch some coke together, and I will clear things up. You see, everyone thinks that there is some kind of entity upstairs, that someone is watching over us and so on… But this is not true. The only thing we know for sure is that our hearts 'beat', and of those beats we only have a certain number. Anyone who has ever played in a band knows that someone needs to keep the beat going! And no one can keep a beat going like Charlie Mingus. What I am trying to say is there is no god! Just Mingus up there in the sky, keeping the beat for us."

I looked over, and he had fallen asleep again, with the lines poring over the Mingus CD case I was listening to.

"Wake the fuck up, you rotten, pathetic wannabe Nazi swine," I screamed!

He busted about, and the coke was gone.

"That's what you get for being a Monkey."

"What, me?"

"Yes, you, now get your shit together. I need to stop for fuel, find out where the fuck we are!"

I stopped at the next service station, took a piss, and got

really high! As I came back to the car, Monkey was full and awake; by 'full', I mean full of some liquor he had just bought! I got into the car again, and Monkey told me he had good news and bad news.

"Give me the good news first," I said.

"Well, the good news is we are just two hours away from the farm, our destination."

"And the bad?"

"I found this in my pocket!"

He opened his fist and in it was a strip of acid; it had been a while since I had taken any LSD. Yet my brain did not even take that into consideration. I looked at the street, started the car and said to him out of the corner of my mouth, not yet, when we get to the farm!

The roads were getting stranger, more desert-like with some weary bushes here and there. Monkey gets a phone call on his mobile, murmurs a few 'okays' and 'sure, you got its' into the phone and hangs up.

"Who was that?" I asked.

"Your brother!" he said.

"What did he say?" I asked.

"He said he is not going to be there until the morning." Monkey said.

"Be where?" I asked.

"On the farm, the night belongs to us!" he replied.

I knew that it was a calling from below to munch on the acid he had in his pocket. With a swift move, he grabs the strip, tears two off it and throws it into his mouth. I wasn't about to tolerate a Monkey on acid without having my own peanuts to throw at him.

"Where's mine? I said.

He gave me a strange look but didn't hesitate, ripped two off, and I stuck them on my tongue.

"How much time do we have left?" I asked.

"About twenty-five minutes to the farm," he said

"I meant until the acid kicks in, but that's also important news," I said.

"Oh, ahhhmmmm, maybe fifteen or maybe thirty minutes, depending on whatever the fuck you believe in nowadays. Oh right, depending on when Mingus wills!" he said with a smirk on his face.

The sun was setting behind us as we drove into the farm, and I parked the car and got out. Once I closed the door behind me, I felt a wave of some sorts, a touch of my own senses, scribbling out of me, just to play with the colours appearing amongst the many olive trees yet to dance in fiery beauty as I look for my dignity and mind amongst them.

I woke up the next day, somewhere I could not explain to be a familiar place. It was in the middle of the afternoon. I had toothpaste all over my head, face and arms. The sun was burning down, although I was underneath the shade of an olive tree. I could barely move, there were bruises and sores all over my legs. My shoes were next to me, and I put them on, put my hands above my forehead and stepped out of the shade of the olive tree to have a look around. My eyes hurt. I needed more rest… I don't remember how I got there; all I could feel was the acid slowly crawling away and a dire need to find the car, so I could get some more heroin to run through my body. My nose was running already!

I started walking up the hill. I figured if I had wandered off last night, it must have been downhill; you tend to take the easy way if everything is moving and upside down from acid. After a while, I saw smoke and some run-down cabins I remembered from the farm last time I was here. I was on the right path. The car I had driven here was a baby blue colour, and it was straight ahead of me between some trees. I ran to it, found my stash and for the first time that afternoon, I felt alive and well. Now I just had to find Monkey and my brother.

I got out of the car and got a whiff of burning wood. As I followed the smell, I got closer to what seemed to be Monkey lying next to a fire that must have been still burning a little bit from last night. I gave him a few kicks, and he rolled over; I could see that he was also covered in toothpaste. His eyes were half open as I asked him what the toothpaste was all about. He said it was my idea of protecting us from the heat in the morning, but he couldn't really remember the details either. I got him a few beers out of the car, and he slowly came to himself.

"Where is my brother?" I asked.

"He left already. Me and him took the stuff out of the car earlier this morning, then he left, and I went back to sleep!" Monkey said.

I was upset that my brother didn't wait to have some words with me, but apparently, he had something more important to do. Beside the fact that he didn't want to see me all runny-nosed and strung out.

"But he left us instructions," Monkey said.

"What do you mean?" I asked.

"He talked to your father, and we are to take some of the old equipment to him," he said.

"To my father?" I asked.

"Yeah, now!" he said.

"That is the last place I needed to drive to in my condition," I said.

"It is what it is," he says and opens up another beer.

The equipment we had brought down was for my older brother to grow weed; it was his new business idea. He was always looking for ways to make money; someone had to find ways to put bread on the table, I sure as fuck never did. I packed some of the old stuff my father needed into the car, then went behind some bushes and made sure to get really fucking high! Then got back into the car.

It took us a good day's drive to get to the region where my father was living at the time; Monkey was asleep the whole drive. I, on the other hand, was a mess! I had been talking to myself the whole ride trying to keep myself from crying. My nerves were at a dead end. My head was spinning around between my childhood memories of the abuse my father had put us through, and all the other events frozen in my head. I was in a cage, stuck in the weave of time, screaming at myself for repeating my father's addiction myself. The hour before we got to where he lived was the most difficult hour of my life. The past I declared to be mine and the longing for a father who never existed was dripping down on my soul. All the sweat parts I remember are just stories I tell myself!

"Wake up, Monkey, we are here!" I said.

"What?" he asked.

"We are at my dad's place," I said.

"How fast did you drive?" he asked.

"That is a question you wouldn't need to ask if you had been awake," I said.

"Let's get the stuff out of the car," he said.

"Okay," I replied.

I was calmer than I had been in the car… I don't know why. Maybe it was the calm before the storm. I knocked on the door, my father, with his long grey hair, opened it. There was some stuff to carry in, so I just whistled a 'hallo' and got on with the show. After settling in, I went into the living room where my father had everything out already; he had probably been smoking spliff after spliff waiting for us, complaining, because to him, everything we did for him was always later than scheduled. Monkey came in with him a good ten minutes later, after they had stored everything in the garage. Monkey sat down on the couch and opened a beer.

I was in the middle of the living room at the coffee table, and Monkey, sat next to me on the couch, had already finished the beer. He opened another one, and my father came in and sat down next to me. I had just finished rolling a joint as my father started to make his own. He looked at me and said…

"How was the drive?"

"Okay," I said.

"All of it? Spain as well?" he asked.

"Yeah, most of it. Oh, by the way, here's the money, the 200 euros!" I said.

I had brought him 200 euros from my brother, so he could pay his rent or something or other.

"Thank you. Where is your brother at the moment?" he asked.

"He had business to attend to in Spain. I didn't even get to see him," I said.

"He is still down there?" he asked.

"Yes," I said.

"I thought he was back already. He didn't come back with you?" he asked.

"No," I said.

"I never know what your older brother is up to nowadays.

He is always getting less and less shit done than he is supposed to," he said.

"What did you just say?" I asked.

"Well, your brother…" he stated.

"What about him," I asked.

"Seems to me he never gets anything done!" he said.

I don't exactly remember the look on my father's face as he said those last words, but it was enough to get me to explode. In a fraction of a second, I turned the coffee table in front of us over on his head. While all the belongings on it flew about and were still in the air, my fists were already clenched and flew towards his face before anything hit the ground. I went off on him and struck his face with the ugliest words coming out of my mouth.

"You rotten junkie, son of a cunt, fuck you and all the bullshit you put us through!" I shouted.

Monkey grabbed me, and for a second or two I was separated from his face. I wiggled my way out of Monkey's arms only to fly at his face again. This time I was aiming and hitting every body part my father had; my arms couldn't swing at him fast enough.

"IT WAS YOUUU, YOU WHO PUT US THROUGH THE GRINDING MILL, YOU WHO LEFT US, YOU THE SCUM OF THIS FORSAKEN HISTORY YOU CALL A FAMILY. I SHOULD BURY YOU ONCE AND FOR ALL!" I screamed at him.

Monkey watched in awe for a few seconds until he had to step in. He had never seen this side of me. I was a peaceful man. I usually tended to hurt myself and not others.

This time he was not going to let me slip away. He dragged me out of the room all the way to the steps in front of the house. I couldn't breathe; I had blood all over my clothes and hands. My tears were running, and all I had was Monkey's face in front of me, who just didn't know if he should call my brother for help or maybe an ambulance, because by the look of it, my father wasn't moving.

He went inside, came out really quickly and said to me, "Clean yourself up and get the car started. We need to take him to a hospital."

I washed up, got into the car, and Monkey carried my father in.

I couldn't look at him; on one hand, I just wasn't ready, and I still needed time to work through what I had just done. I drove up to the hospital, and we got him in there as fast as we could. European hospitals are much more liberal than American ones; you can't just drag someone to an American hospital all beaten and bloody without answering a fuck load of questions, even if he is your father. The hospital we took him to didn't ask me anything; they didn't even want to start concerning themselves with the farfetched idea that someone's son would do this to his own father and then drive him to a hospital. I signed some papers, and they took him off to a room.

Monkey stayed in the car, he didn't want them to start asking what a drunk German fellow has to do with all this. So the endeavour was all mine to enjoy. I went outside and lit a cigarette. After taking a few drags, I could see that Monkey was sitting in the car that was still parked in front of the hospital. I wanted to get into the car, but something stopped me; I couldn't take a step towards the car. I threw the half-smoked cigarette to the ground. I don't know what it was that made me go back inside the hospital, but I did. The truth is I suffered enough in my youth; all of us did on the injustice law my father ruled with when we grew up as little kids. I just had to get one good long look at him lying there in that hospital bed. Unconscious and without one sparkle in his body. Not only to see my masterpiece signed and all but just to see him in grave danger and severe pain. And so it was.

Chapter 6

Solace Yet to Come

I hate America for making me love it. We fled well from my father. My mother's action of packing in front of him and making him watch us leave went through well. It had a certain effect on him that no one could really anticipate. Such an effect that he even drove us to the airport. He was quiet in the car; he knew that we were leaving *him* and not really Europe. It was as if one side of my father was left with a bitter aftertaste and another with the feeling that he could now indulge in more drug use in a more solitary way. Having a family watch him all those years was too much for him. Even a monster does not like to look in the mirror too often.

In America, we had four uncles on my mom's side living in a house big enough so there would be space for all of us. And so it was we arrived in New York at JFK airport on a normal sunny day. We had seen enough sunny days, but normal was a new phenomenon. One of my uncles picked us up; all four of them were cab drivers and, although they didn't work in New York, they still knew their way around the city. We got into the car and drove south; my siblings and I were in a complete 'volume shock'. We had enough culture shocks behind us, but America is the land of 'big things'. In comparison to Europe we were living in an oversized wonderland now.

All four of us, including my mom, who could not stop

smiling, were looking out the windows. My mother hadn't seen her brothers in a very long time. After the war and fleeing the city where I was born, we split, and everyone chose a different direction. We headed for Europe and the rest well... most of them headed for America. She had never had that smile on her face. For the first time ever, I understood why my mother dealt with things the way she did back then. She had to be tough in front of my father; she had to take things with a grain of salt. She had to grow a shell, which was slowly disappearing. We were a good hour south of the big apple when my mother looked back at us; our heads were still projected towards the world outside. I felt her looking at us, and I turned my head and saw a look on her face I couldn't describe to anyone, not because it's so difficult but simply because there are no words for the beauty she had dripping from her face. I felt safe.

We arrived later that evening; it was just two states south of New York. The east coast of America is a wonderful landscape. There is a lot of precious natural green stuff in America. However, the east coast is special. One Native American river, fall, reserve or plain after the other, it was as if the Native Americans had cursed this land with a paradoxical beauty before they were rotted out by the pilgrims and puritans. It was truly a land of paradox, the most pretty cascading Indian summer sky and the driest concrete full of gasoline-smelling parking lots. The richest, the poorest, the most white, the most black.

The house we arrived at was big. It had nothing but a green forest surrounding it and behind the house was a large wooden terrace. I never in my life had seen before or since the privacy and peace one had surrounding that house, a big chunk of my heart still slumbers in those woods behind that kind house. We settled in the basement, which was large enough for us. My two other brothers and I got one room while my sister got her own. My mother slept in the basement living room. I was the youngest, barely ten years old. We were shy at first, but our uncles made that go away quite quickly. They were full of joy just to have us there. We had, for the first time ever, space to breathe.

America is a land where you can get lost by just staring into the sky! We lived way down in the stick of the hick, real country; we needed that. My mother wasn't the most superstitious woman, but she believed what she herself called the bridges of karma. That evil actions bear evil fruit, this she always said, was a law of the universe. She knew even back then, in that lion's den we once called home back in Europe, that one day that bridge would be crossed. The time we spent there in America continued in this fashion, we had a warm atmosphere. We were together trying to find earth to put our feet upon as a family. Every now and then, treacherous memories would find their way into my system, although unfaithful and perfidious, they would whisper, long before they would be taken and revised as my past.

I was too young to work through them; they were just there. In a kind of slumber yet to be awakened. I trusted in my uncles. I knew them to be men and not monsters. My first years in high school were ones filled with new things. An American high school is a special system, loyal to only the American way and culture. No Hollywood scenario can overexaggerate the 'realm' called high school. It is exactly like they portray it. A haven for sport-driven, hierarchy-hungry kids filled with puberty and sugar. Right in the middle of that, you had the odd teacher or two who really cared, which made it all the better for me. All you need is one diamond in the rough to get my attention. I didn't take much liking to the whole system in general there. I was happy to have it, but I had my own demons calling me; even in those young years, I knew that solace is a fruit you can only reap after years of sowing the seed.

My first battlefield was the scorn echoing in the back of my mind. The years in high school were nice, and the years in the woods where I would spend most of my time. They were continuing to grow into a struggle nonetheless. America is bitter and tough on immigrants. It takes money to really live in luxury, and that we did not have. My mother tried her hand at a few jobs here and there, but it never held long until she was fired or replaced. She was too old to keep up. She was an academic woman with no time left after raising four kids on her own. The minute my older brother could, he went to work so we could make ends meet.

And so it was for the next years, my brother broke his back, so we had what we needed, and I would spend time trying to grow up normal. My mother was addicted to the radio; she loved the news. During those years, I must have soaked up half of the world's events. At night, she would watch movies and between the morning to the afternoon, when the radio got good, she would read her books. The woman could read like no one could. She didn't have a specific genre; she would read anything she got her hands on. For birthdays or any other occasions, she would always take us to a museum or just to the library. She did the best she could. And her best sufficed to a supernatural level. The woman was a pillar of strength and knowledge during those years in America. I learned in those years how to be a man, not from four uncles, not from some other TV figure or even the men I would make up as imaginary figures just to soothe the longing I had for a father. I learned it from my mother, the most sublime woman and just mind that was ever created by Mr. Mingus himself!

Chapter 7

Do Not Follow the Rabbit, Do Not Go Down the Rabbit Hole. Forget the Rabbit and Dig Your Own Hole!

We left America when I was a twenty-year-old man, a good ten years we spent there. After deciding to leave due to my mother's illness, no doctor could explain to us what was going on inside her body, but they were able to make it much worse. It was a horrible struggle trying to get free help in America. Let alone the distance you have to travel just to get Medicare. So it didn't take us long to yet again decide to cross the Atlantic Ocean and go back to Europe, where help was much more abundant.

    We settled in a different city from where my father was living. My mother's condition turned into a stable one due to the healthcare system that existed there. It was familiar to us, the exchange of culture didn't shock us anymore, and we weren't running away from anyone; this time, we were seeking medical refuge for my mother. I was a young man back then, and my memory serves me well. In that regard, I spent a lot of time travelling. I wanted to see everything, and so it was for the next years.

    Changing continents only gives you so much time until your past catches up with you. Especially if parts of your history start in the place you have now revisited. The body travels much faster than the mind does; our thoughts were still in America, and between us, we still spoke in English. I can't tell you why, that was just the way it was. Those years in America were the most peaceful. Although my mother got sick there and still was, it was a different battle. One could reconcile the destiny brought upon by above, much easier. Yes, this made us sad, but we went on with life. Like I said, my mother was more or less stable.

Don't ask me why this happened to my mother and not to the rotten junkie who calls himself my father. If there is a god, then one of these days, he will walk up to the stands to accept his Oscar for the longest-running satire series ever produced in showbusiness, life. With the international record for the most re-runs ever.

I was about twenty-five years old when I decided to get a cat. I already had a name for her; it definitely needed to be a female cat, and her name would be Hiroshima, don't ask why; I just liked the name, me and my roommate at the time called her Hiroshi. It turned out that my roommate had an allergy to cats; he was unaware of it, so we decided to part ways. I had just met this girl who wasn't living far from where my apartment was. So I gave her a call. The phone didn't ring twice before she picked it up.

"Yello," she answered.
"Hey, it's me. How are you?" I said.
"Good, thanks, and you?" she replied.
"All right," I said.
"You back in town?" she asked.
"Yeah, since a few months now," I said.
"What's up?" she asked.
"Do you have space for me in your apartment?" I asked.
"Only you or your cat as well?" she said.
"Both of us, of course," I said.
"When are you coming?" she asked.

"Now?" I ventured.
"Tomorrow is better," she said.
"Then I will see you tomorrow," I said.
"Okay," she said.

I didn't have many belongings, a guitar, some records and my wardrobe. I got everything ready and decided to celebrate by smoking some coke. I had learned how to back in the States. It was one of the first drugs I consumed, it was never my favourite, but it was something I did for special occasions, and this seemed like the right time. I still had a bag full of some powder coke from some festival I went to in the summer. It was autumn now, and the autumn season was my favourite, everything seemed just to fit in place. I cooked, made a pipe out of a plastic bottle and took some hits. It was a kind of leaving ritual, so I didn't cook everything, hid the rest somewhere and decided to properly end the ritual with a big joint that would send me to sleep.

The next day, in the morning, while I was drinking my coffee, with everything packed and ready to leave, I turned on the radio just as my cup of coffee was half-empty and Leonard Cohen's 'Dance me to the end of love' was playing on a radio station, everything felt perfect. I finished my coffee, got my cat into the box to move her in and said goodbye to the apartment. It was a new start for me, and it barely took me a few hours to move; her place was just around the corner. After I settled in and let my cat out of her travel cage, I went into my room and decided to unpack my belongings.

The apartment she lived in was a cat's paradise. I never felt like a person anyway, so I felt at home there. The kitchen was small but full of hanging things. There were three tree stumps in it, one in the corner and two in the middle serving as support for the sink where they were rigged underneath. Stacks of old books and magazines were on the old but beautiful table next to the wall, across from the sink. All kinds of toys and half statue-like things everywhere. I loved the place immediately.

A few months passed, and we grew to be lovers, me and my roommate. We both came from immigrant parents, and we both had voices telling us what to do and not to do; we both had demons we loved and hated. The truth was we both loved and hated our own selves! However, together where solitude suddenly turned into something you could share with another person, we were together but always alone. It was worth gold to me this new adventure.

My ritual of smoking coke through a bottle was turning into a weekly thing, and I slowly felt the need to share it with somebody. I didn't want to ask her. I knew that at one point, she would either ask what I would do in my room so often or just come in and catch me on the pipe. Which was kind of the farce I was looking for. It was going to be New Year soon, and we had planned to have some friends over, so I got equipped, meaning I went to a friend and snatched some acid from him. Fireworks just work way better when there is some LSD involved. Our friends came over about ten o'clock at night, my roommate and I decided to eat the acid right as they were coming in the door so we would be at full peak or near it when the fireworks began.

We went out as a group of six people and waited for the show to begin. My phone rang, but I didn't want to answer it until the fireworks and most of the acid were gone. We waited out on the street until the clock hit midnight. Our heads were in full throttle when those fireworks hit. I looked at her; she was a good five meters down the footpath. Once I got closer to her, I could see that she was pointing to the sky as if she was counting something with her fingers. With my shoulder next to hers, I could see that her finger was pointing up to the fireworks. Up there, we saw together, one Unicorn after the other coming out in majestic uniforms of sparkles from the smoke the fireworks would leave behind. They melted together with the clouds up there. They rolled together only to be spawned anew by the next generation of magic dust exploding behind them. Everyone saw it, but we felt something. Something rise in us. Something I could not explain as being alive, whatever it was, it had made space in both of us, for from that day on, we were officially Unicorns stuck in human bodies.

Once we got back home after hours of partying somewhere, I saw that my cell phone had a bunch of missed calls. I looked at it and saw that my older brother must have called me ten times at least. With all the acid just leaving my head, I called him back, and he answered right away. His voice was very awkward and silent.

"Can you come over?" he asked.
"Sure, where are you?" I replied.
At Mom's place!" he said.
"Okay," I said.
"Just get in a cab and come over, please!" he said.

I took the next cab I could and got out at my mother's apartment. I rang the bell, and my two brothers and my sister were there. One of them buzzed me in. I didn't hear which one. The minute they opened the door, I knew, I knew that my mother had passed. It was morning, I was up all night, yet I had to have a look at her. She was laying on the couch where she would always drink her tea and read her books. My dear mother passed on that morning; she lay with half a smile on her face in a calm horizontal sway. She looked to the sky and was finally happy!

The End